In Cumbria

John Watson
In Cumbria

In Cumbria
ISBN 978 1 76041 276 0
Copyright © text John Watson 2017

First published 2017 by
GINNINDERRA PRESS
PO Box 3461 Port Adelaide 5015 Australia
www.ginninderrapress.com.au

Contents

Beyleful	7
The Game of Tanka	33
Leah Lee	37
Domestic Outpourings, Particularly of Tea	47
In Cumbria	65

Beyleful

1

All that follows is derived
From the patchwork of memoirs of Henri Beyle
All written, as was his life, in transit.

When he was seven his mother died.
Seven years had formed stalactites,
Slow carbonates congesting his chest;

She it was whom he had wanted to embrace
And kiss endlessly, always on her breast
Which should ideally be naked.

2

In the Louvre he encountered
Gérard's *Psyche and Cupid*
And was reminded of many women,

But none was like this girl,
Beet-sugar-sweet and pale,
Clearly and beautifully reluctant

To adopt the role of 'complete woman',
Instead looking into the future
With a kind of provisional regret

Lest it should ever eventuate
And displace all she presently loved.
The boy, equally childish, smooth-skinned

And with unconvincing wings –
Touching her ear, impossibly chaste,
Was almost as tentative as she.

Outside the Louvre in the sunlit world
He asked: Is any man or any woman ever
As reticent or gentle as these two?

3

The smooth-skinned youth unassertively
Whispering at her forehead,
She was very much inclined to remain,
If not 'languidly frozen in time'
Then at least wondering how to return
From her viridian hill without walking;
Just so Méthilde (q.v.) would in years to come
Allow Beyle only a cool reception
Once a month, for tea, in her dining room.

4

Alexandrine with whom he failed (physically)
Was superb, imperious, not derisive,
But did decline his offer of remedy.

This failure contrasted strangely
With his many Ovidian sevenfold successes.
Failure with Alexandrine was (alas) broadcast

By another officer present in the brothel and became
(In a figure not from Shakespeare, his idol)
An albatross about his reputation.

5

Failure with the courtesan Alexandrine encouraged
His distaste for romantic poetry,
Which would soon devolve into the Symbolist school,

And advanced his decision to write fiction
Which would be truthful and self-effacing
And entirely free from Alexandrines.

6

In the context of mythic time
From which she has reluctantly emerged
To arrive at this viridian hill

Psyche (see above)
May well be thinking *the pleasure brief
And the position ridiculous,*

Prefiguring thus, in Beyle's fruitless pursuit
Of Méthilde Viscontini Dembowski
Her preference for afternoon tea.

7

Psyche is as immobile as the valley behind her.
Her cloak gathered in folds under her
Is an exquisite chestnut. Rolled below her waist

The transparent gauze challenges the painter.
Cupid is scarcely less feminine or supple;
Both are intent on posing for the future.

8

The rose-ice figures of Psyche and Cupid
With their forearms in tableau
Seem to arrange themselves as a monogram

Such as Beyle described in the sand
At Lake Albano, mysteriously
Delineating there all the entwining loves of his life.

9

His failures and successes
Are perhaps encapsulated
In this exercise in contrary motion:

The aristocratic Giulia Rinieri,
Virgin of nineteen years
Addressed him thus:

'I am perfectly aware
That you are old and unbeautiful –
And yet –', then kissed him. Hesitant

For several months, he then
Slept with her, after which
She declined his offer of marriage.

10

And again, Alberthe de Rubempré was married,
Was in love with the occult
And, only after that, with Beyle.

He loved her for 'a month at most'
Then after his death she tried
To summon the shade of 'poor Henri'

But poor Henri was altogether then
Too pragmatic, too much the realist,
To appear in such a scenario.

11

All the while Countess Clémentine Curial
Could be sensed moving in the ballroom above,
For three days he lived in a dark cellar

And waited for her to bring by candlelight –
Whenever she could elude her husband –
Food and the orchestrations of her body.

12

Méthilde in Milan! The cathedral frescoes,
Their four thousand columns, the summer solstice –
Méthilde! Carriages outside the Opera

Where the men milling on horseback
(Absent Méthilde!) address the white-bosomed
Ladies in coaches leaning from windows…

Méthilde! That mellifluous happiness
And the envelopment of love, alas
Drained of meaning by her indifference.

13

In Milan cathedral, overwhelmed
By its orchard of dove-grey columns,
Again and again he saw Méthilde

And in this theatre of white noise
Saw her as one of the many Louvre Venuses
Although Sunday service was scarcely the time or place.

14

Milan is set in a forest like an island
Round which flows a vacant sea –
The vacancy of desolate love.

Mozart! Shakespeare! All attainable,
But Méthilde is always beyond reach!
The clarity of Mozart, the all-encompassing

Presence of Shakespeare – both these
Prefigured in Méthilde's beautiful face
But, alas, not offering themselves there –

She who even at a Mozart opera
Seems distracted, protecting something ephemeral,
And who has never read Shakespeare.

15

Retreating with Napoleon's blighted forces
Through the bitter snows of regret

There was little time and many an hour
To think as he had thought so long

In childhood of his aunt's white, glimpsed,
Separating thighs descending from a carriage.

16

Later crossing the Alps, he existed in a state
Of exhilarated happiness, which seemed
Inexplicably dispensed by the landscape

Passing but changing only slowly.
Nothing seemed to supervene. The sky,
The diamond necklace of surrounding peaks,

The undidactic presence of snow – everything
Resigned to be itself yet proselytising,
Allowed space for irretrievable thoughts

The more to be valued for being so…
And recollection at several removes
Of the face of Méthilde Viscontini Dembowski.

17

'The gravestone I would leave in Milan
Would celebrate Mozart, Shakespeare and love
– There is little else worthy of record

Since Méthilde is Russia encountered in snow
And retreated from without attainment,
Leaving the Moscow citadel unoccupied –

The stone might read,
Henri Beyle: Milanese: He lived:
He wrote: He loved.'

18

Sunlight on river slurry, bridge towers,
Skies perpetually unconfiding, the uncleared forest,
Milan cathedral more dense with riches than Rome,

Water in shivering peaks with the sirocco,
Lines of infantry still winding down a corridor
With Russian snows forlornly far behind,

The great expanse already shone as remotely,
And almost as fictive in memory,
As the face of Méthilde.

19

Rowing all day with swallows
On the unreflecting face of Lake Maggiore

In every disappearing oar gulf he saw
Just as she had eluded him so many times

The retreating face of Méthilde Dembowski
As much like sky as water.

20

In 1800 Stendhal
(As he now had become)
Fell in free-fall
In love with Angelina Pietragrua
Virtuous married Milanese *pietra dura*
Inlaid but unlaid.
In 1811

They met again. This time
She crossed that bridge when he came to it.
He went to a professional seamstress:
'I am celebrating a triumph.
I want these suspenders embroidered
(As one does) with the following:
AP 22 September 1811.'

21

Set against this embroidered triumph
Was the love, plummeting in vain,

For Méthilde Dembowski,
Which was white silk entirely free of texts.

22

In Shakespeare's *Lover's Complaint*
Beyle marks lines 15-17:
Oft did she heave her napkin to her eyne
Which on it had conceited characters
Laund'ring the silken figures in the brine.

He remarks to another officer
On adjacent horseback in Russian snows
That because of the way in which words
Have become more prosaic in subsequent centuries
No one could again write as beautifully.

23

Paris has no mountains. This,
He believes, is its only fault.
That Paris has no mountains rubs salt
In the wound of his disconsolateness.

In Italy, towns like Milan
(But what town is like Milan?) look
Towards the mountains. Clouds shake
Light in our faces like spring rain.

24

And Milanese women are as beautiful
And sublimely at their ease
And endlessly elusive as the close
In Bach's long delayed cadences.

25

The modulations of Bach
Lost for two centuries under stale candlewax,
The operas of Mozart and Cimarosa,
The hundreds of columns in the Milan cathedral
Similarly similar and dissimilar,

The advancing mountain in clear weather,
The subtleties of colour distant and close
Each with its own breath and presence –
All of these are emblems of the beauty
Of the women criss-crossing Milan.

26

In a dazzlement of sunlight he remembered again:

For three days he lived in a cellar
Warmed only by candlelight
And the visits with food

And the loosening gown
And orchestrations and bestowals
Of Countess Clémentine Curial.

27

The endlessly prolonged cadence
In certain harpsichord pieces of Bach,

The impression on approaching Milan
That the forest is impenetrable,

The moment in a Mozart opera
When gaiety becomes sadness

Are, despite their pervasiveness, of no account
Compared with his recollections of Méthilde's face.

28

He recalls seeing Melanie Guilbert
Bathing naked in a river –
She with whom he lived for a year,

And at once being plunged back into boyhood
Where in gallery after gallery he longed
To bathe amongst the Louvre Venuses.

29

For almost the first time on horseback, in the forest
He strayed from the path and found an empty bird's egg –
From which he imagined the fledgling escaping.
And he remembered a dream he had forgotten,
A dream of entering a new world.

30

'I dreamed we were together once more,
Méthilde and I,
Beside a channel entering the sea
Below a ploughed field sky;

Strangely the sea changed its course
And ran beside rather than towards the cliff;
Méthilde threw off
Her pale silk and waded into the wave.'

31

As a child Henri Beyle,
Stepping beyond the pale of childhood
And being conducted through the Louvre,
Learned to pause before its nudes,
And now strangely at La Scala,
While a Cimarosa aria calmly undulated,
He seemed to see again these bathers
Holding their fans as he resumed his seat.

32

An early indicator of things to come
And of the persistence of memory
Stored from long pauses in the Louvre:

He stops in the street. He is adolescent.
Virginia Kubly, Grenoble actress,
Comes downstage into the public gardens

And he is unable to move, consumed and gazing,
And cannot speak to her.

33

The past is perpetually revisited.
In 1800 Beyle was seventeen.
In Milan, city of overwhelming futures,
He saw Angelina Pietragrua
(Gina), a married woman,

And could not speak of love;
Until again in Italy emerging
After eleven years from the forests of Milan –
(Warning: a salacious traducing follows)
He saw, conquered and came.

34

The pursuit of these assignations
Was to be marked by obstacles
(Nuns sleeping in adjoining rooms,
Children staring in corridors, sheets shaken
At open windows as secret signs,
Gina's indiscretions in church,
Her increasing recklessness) until

The final scene in a gallery
Beside a large bronze *Amor*
With Gina on her knees
Distraught and clinging and crying
That she had never loved him more.

35

This Angelina Pietragrua – of flashing eyes
And flesh as firm as her name's stone
And passions widening like stone circles in water

Had always ridden the waves,
While, contrariwise, Méthilde
Was always a ship passing in the night.

36

Adele Rebuffel, the child aged 12,
Whose mother did not rebuff him
Was like Gérard's Psyche in childhood.
Descending from the boudoir with *maman*,
He would meet Adele's solemn gaze.

For four years he dreamt of her
Watching her open like a rare flower
Seeing there the mysterious essence of her mother.
Descending from the boudoir with *maman*
He would see Adele calmly reading.

For four years in the same house
And descending from the boudoir with *maman*
He saw her curious gaze. During this time
As if anticipating Rohmer's *Contes Morales*
Only once his hand grazed her breast.

37

Unfulfilled loves passed him with the profusion
Of choruses flooding the box at La Scala
Or the façade columns at the Milan cathedral:

Wilhemina von Griesheim (Minette),
Alexandrine Duru, wife of his cousin Pierre,
And of course, most painful of unconsummations,

Méthilde Viscontini Dembowski.
Others were as fleeting as scene changes;
Only Méthilde remained motionless in the footlights.

38

Seeing through a keyhole one sultry day
Gina in slow rotation with another man

He found them 'like puppets dancing'
And felt less regret for the eleven years of waiting.

39

Abstracted by reverie, fleeing
One humid day from the past
Which had devolved into fantasies

And positing the possibility at least
Of certainty or tangible reality,
The solidity of the present

As it might be embodied
In the embrace of a woman,
He awaited the arrival of the sirocco.

Outside the Milan cathedral
The breeze increased – as if
It too were escaping the past,

And the entire day seemed to slow,
Fretted and braided in its progress
Like Psyche resisting the persuasions of Cupid.

40

Faded rose stucco, palms, the oddity
Of a single deciduous tree amongst others,
The grey green of olive leaves,

The feminine arms of a wayward eucalypt,
The *passeggiata* seeming to dissolve
And re-form repeating certain figurations:

Into all this dispersion
Came walking a woman in whom all variety
Had been compressed and made singular: *She*.

41

Rowing on Lake Albano, white
Fluctuations ruffled by oars, memory
Ruffled similarly by the air on his face,

He thought of several women
All in exact particulars,
All now in rooms beyond his reach.

42

On Lake Garda after a boat passes,
'The little waves arrive, speaking –
And I cannot resist noting
This is like the past lingering. Pretentious? *Moi*?

A little after the waves pass
Birds return, or one notices them again;
Sunlight resumes its enjoyment
Of the water and every other incident.'

43

Swallows nesting by the lake
Summarise in arcs
All of his least infatuations,

All of them like cusps
Abruptly abandoned
And swerved from into other arms.

44

'My Dear Friend,

                I am obliged,
As you may see, to sign my letters
With a dozen invented names.
Here in Milan I am apparently
Considered a spy. The Austrian police

Are equally suspicious of my fame.
This morning I resolved reluctantly
To leave Milan.

                I visited Méthilde
To take my leave, she who recently
Decreed that I might visit her
At most once a month
And always in her drawing room.

She seemed affected

                even shedding tears
And said, 'When will you return?'
'Never.' It seemed that I was trudging
Still in deep snow and almost

Without emotion and with Russia
Recently left far behind.
She trembled at the word –
          She
Whom I had loved unrequitedly
From 1818 to 1821.
          I thought
Again of my long-imagined gravestone
Which I desired to be carved
As follows: *Henri Beyle: Milanese: He lived:*
          He wrote: He loved.

45

The unattainable Méthilde Dembowski
Whom once he followed in disguise
(Green spectacles and an overcoat)

Inspired his book *On Love*
With its theory of idealising 'crystallisation'.
It sold 17 copies in its first 10 years.

46

'Disturbed with outreaches of grey
The lake's gold spread like past regrets.

From time to time we heard across the water
Peasants singing on the opposite shore.

The vaporous Italian sun brought silent heat;
A silence which could happily co-exist

With peasants singing on the opposite shore.
A breath of wind from time to time

Disturbed with grey the lake's gold
Like the gold of days when I still pursued Gina.'

47

'Of the fifteen fairest women in Milan,
That I should fall in love and be refused
By Angelina Pietragrua – she whose name
Implies the rapt impenetrability of stone
And to whom after eleven years I have returned.

In this new and prolonged campaign
Conducted with exquisite care, we look
At paintings in the best galleries,
We promenade about the Castello Sforzioto;
I take her to the celebrated echo

In the villa with its walls of water;
We drink coffee in its elegant courtyards;
I rely heavily on our contemplation of *The Last Supper*
At the Church of Santa Maria della Grazie
Until finally the citadel is attained.'

48

'When, after our years together in Marseilles
Melanie Guilbert, actress of many roles,
Returned to Paris, I was alone.

She it was who, in wading naked
Into the silk and crinoline water, restored to me
My childhood and the Louvre bathers.

Under that proscenium arch of lost days
I made my soliloquy which continues to this day:
I, Henri Beyle, find no lasting happiness.'

49

'Like all the bathers attended by demigods,
Rose-white in the Louvre's azure streams,
I saw Melanie entering the water

Revising every notion I had held in youth
Of *white* and *arms raised* and *flow of hair*;

And here she was drawing from me far greater
Accolades than ever covered her on the stage.'

50

'Signor Isimbardi said that he desired
To show me Lake Como – and at
The Caffé del'Accademia asked,
"What is it you expect to find in Rome?
If, as I suspect, it is sublime beauty,
Lake Como is in Nature what the ruins
Of the Colosseum are to architecture,
Correggio's *St Jerome* among pictures –"
And, I thought, Méthilde among women.'

The Game of Tanka

An anthology of a hundred poems from the twelfth century,
Each poem having five lines, constitutes a popular card game
Having a hundred cards, each being the last two lines
Of one of these poems. A creek overrun with willows;
A soughing breeze; shadows. Most players know the poems
By heart. The reader, usually a respected mother
And hostess at the poetry party, leads the game.
She spreads the cards on the woven bamboo.
Facing the players, the reader and convenor
Places another set of cards face down beside her,
Each card containing a whole poem. Cutting the pack,
She takes a card at random and begins to read aloud.

Each player must identify the poem's last two lines
And be the first to seize the card containing these.
Many ladies consider it unwise to wear a kimono
As sleeves are sometimes torn in the players' excitement.
Milk thistle, purple statice, clover, thornbush and willow
May abound in the field beside the game's pavilion.
Passions run high. The playing cards may be frequently
Decorated with portraits – often imaginary or conventional
Of the 100 poets, since nothing is known of many.
There are usually several favourite poems involving
Crickets or grasshoppers or cicadas or swallows, all
Eliciting loud and enthusiastic cries from the players.

These tanka follow strictly the syllable count
As it is required by tradition. Their popularity
In large part depends on this adherence to the past,
Since many a reader and player disapprove of the liberties
Which have increasingly crept into modern practice.
The grammatical shift or caesura or turn
May occur after the second or third line –
And a frisson of disillusion spreads rapidly should any poet
Have failed to observe this. One day in summer heat
When gentlemen have shed coats and the ladies their kimonos
To wear 'dragonfly-wings' or 'gossamers', and cows
Have moved into the shade of cropped mulberry trees,

Several children of the presiding mother interrupt by calling
From the reed pool nearby in which they are wading.
And the game falters when several players lapse into reading poems
Aloud from the cards bearing the full text
And discussing aspects of their exquisite prosody.
Another day – it is the season of the giant hollyhock
Which seems to be stretching and peering in at the window –
There are several Games of the Hundred Poems
Proceeding at the same time in adjacent groups.
One lady in rapt admiration, and exclaiming at once
On recognising an entire poem about a waterfall,
Turns slightly and seizes with excessive zeal

The appropriate card, but from the adjoining game. So great
Is the attention of players there to a bowerbird poem,
Where the bird leaves tracks through snow, that no one notices
And it is not until much later that confusion
Interrupts these games. In a manoeuvre not unlike this,
An egotist poet – that creature tacitly outlawed by poems
In the celebrated and long-standing hundred,
Poems preferring mist and lake cloud and cicada drone
And pines rising steeply from the sea, to the contamination
Of rhetoric or ego – insinuates a fresh set of cards
Printed in similar font with his own poems. This time, however,
The deception is discovered almost at once. Sometimes

The players experience subtle signs of turbulence –
A trembling in the cards relayed to their hands,
A shaking in the pines flanking the lake-house,
A shuddering in the pool where yet no insect
Appears on its surface. This disturbance is puzzling.
But eventually it is traced back to the reader,
Who, in cutting the cards seems repeatedly
To open the pack at perhaps the youngest
And most beautiful of the contributing poets still living,
So that the players realise with both startlement
And irresistible certainty that the mother
Is profoundly infatuated with this young fabulist.

Further contingencies add oddity. One day a poem
Is found by unanimous agreement to be so beautiful
As to demand a complete suspension of the game;
On another occasion one player, by some sort of reversion
Into childhood appears to regard the game as some
Confused version of the game of Snap – and in a confusion
Of cicadas sounding outside the veranda, and other voices
Evoked in the enunciated lines, seizes all the cards.
Once a deranged player calls, 'I'll see your curlew
Singing before dawn, and raise you two flowering tulip-trees';
And, one afternoon, poetic ardour grows so strongly
That the mother proposes playing the game without cards.

This is the signal for the tea ceremony.
The reader has put the cards to one side
And absents herself. The players continue to enthuse,
Reciting texts in turn without recourse to the cards,
Until the mother returns with one of her children
Transporting the tray with the tea.
Now begins a process as complicated with order
As the conventions governing the disposition of syllables
And the choice of dragonfly and oriole and moon
And insect and fretted butterfly wing in the texts.
On such occasions the game is never quite abandoned
But the taking of tea supplants for a period its variations.

Leah Lee

1881: Laforgue arrived
In Berlin as
Reader of French

To the Empress
Augusta of Germany.
For five years

He was employed,
Largely in Berlin,
Diligent but bored,

And, in lieu
Of anything else,
Wrote more verse:

Grotesqueries of Pierrot;
Clowns; metaphysical obliquities;
A prose *Hamlet*,

As sardonically unShakespearean
Man about Elsinore
Mocking all expectations;

Andromeda, an unOvidian
'Wild, pubescent girl';
Excursions into curiosity

At collisions between
Sublime and mundane,
Anatomical and animistic.

Bemused by snow
He was also
Amused to note

Amongst many oddities
The dual function
Of the penis –

What a sublime
Sense of humour
God's non-existence manifested.

Visiting music halls
In Berlin, writing
Vers increasingly *libre*,

Skating for hours,
Doing figure eights
Surrounded by girls,

One English girl
Calling in pirouettes
Across the ice,

Yours, yours, yours,
Contradicting his belief
In three sexes:

Men, and women,
And English girls,
The latter inviolate,

Whom he thought
'The only creatures
Not easily undressed.'

Although he was
Probably the first
Poet to use

The word *clitoris*
In a poem,
He was wary

Of its bearers.
Despite the mystery
Of English girls

He studied English
With one. She
Was Leah Lee.

One photograph exists
Showing her face
In a halo

Or perhaps, hat,
And looking strangely
Like young Rimbaud.

She is twenty-four,
A year younger
Than he. She

Seems reticent yet
A forthright teacher.
After several lessons

He proposed diffidently
That they might
Visit the Museum.

She blushed and
Lowered her head.
Later he apologised.

Then she agreed
And they began
An implicit courtship.

Sometimes he sent
An opera ticket
As if unwanted

Only to appear
In the seat
Unexpectedly beside her.

One evening after
A ravishing concert
He hesitantly made

A 'circumlocutious proposal'.
She returned with
'An extraordinary look'.

They shook hands
Avoiding eye contact,
Not yet kissing.

He described her
To friends as
'Impossible to describe' –

Her baby face,
Her malicious smile,
Her large eyes,

Her funny accent,
Her charming French.
He called her

'My little personage'
But she had
A persistent cough

And should not
Remain in Berlin
For another winter.

September 30, 1886.
The engaged couple
Meet in Liège

And by train
Travel to Brussels
Spending the night

('In circumstances unknown')
Before reaching Calais
Where Leah leaves

By steam ferry
For England. He
Returned to Paris.

They had planned
To marry on
New Years Eve

But Laforgue (writing
To his sister)
Protested his poverty

And was frantically
Seeking employment, or
Publication of *Hamlet,*

Or a loan,
None of which
Happened. Somehow loans

From family estates
In Montevideo, Uruguay
(Laforgue's birth place)

Arrived in time.
Thus he secured
A Paris apartment;

On December 30,
Taking the train
He reached England

And next morning
He met Leah
And they married

At St Barnabas,
Kensington. The ceremony
Took 15 minutes.

Celebrating their bliss
They drank tea
Like true natives.

Three days later
The couple travelled
To wintry Paris.

Laforgue was ill
With a cold
Lasting three months.

But despite this
Leah was continually
'Gay and whimsical' –

When friends visited
The modest apartment
They were greeted

By a fire,
A beautiful lamp,
A fragrant tea,

From the service
Given to him
By the Empress.

But by now
He was often
Bedridden for days;

He took opium
Every other night
To suppress coughing.

The doctor advised
That only sun
Might cure him.

Leah was cheerful
And so funny
With short hair.

She was patient
And always present.
August 16th was

His 27th birthday;
Leah was 26.
On August 20th

He said suddenly
To his brother,
Emile, recently summoned,

And to Leah
Who looked pale,
'I think I'm

Hallucinating.' And then
In five minutes
It was over.

Leah now disappears
From the record
For several months;

Then in December
The following year
A letter reached

A literary friend.
'My dear Sir,
I am leaving

For Menton. Could
You kindly visit
On a matter

Concerning my husband's
Papers and manuscripts?'
The following day

She handed over
A suitcase filled
With Laforgue's manuscripts.

Then she left
For sunny Menton.
But her health

Continued to decline.
Soon after entering
A London convent

In June 1888
Tuberculosis reunited her
With her husband.

Domestic Outpourings, Particularly of Tea

1

The morning tea morning is as still as –
Still persisting with this worn out
Simile distillery? Well,

There should be no problem just as long
As outside, the actual morning
Is rightly seen as a well,

Holding far more than could be ever
Ladled and poured into tea cups.
And isn't it true that anecdote

Far out-trumps description? For instance,
That when Keats was writing Hyperion
A cricket ball blackened his eye?

And no amount of description of the view
From the tea ceremony veranda
With or without similes could compete?

2

The blackbirds in adjacent fields
Answer each other across our helicopter bubble
Where we take tea and wait admiringly
To hear their tissue paper curled streamers.

3

We like a man who's tardy with his emails;
It's something like – this spaciousness –
The spaces between a) the pouring of tea,
b) the resumption of the lawn's landscape
And c) subsequent sips from cooling cups.

4

During the taking of tea
With milk and no sugar
Someone pours recitations

From the *Book of Anecdotes*.
One: Psychiatrist to woman
Dressed as Napoleon:

'It's a pity, Mrs Brancourt,
You didn't consult me sooner,
Before the Battle of Waterloo.'

5

Pouring tea in sunlight
With its apotheosis of dapple

Is like Marianne Moore sleeping
Until the age of sixty

With her overshadowing mother
Who often strongly denounced

Her lines as 'prosaic' –
While nonetheless Marianne

Managed spectacular sleep
With panoramic REM

And saw round corners
By counting syllables.

6

A vase of roses in another room
Just out of sight
                   beyond the door ajar –
When is a door not a door?

Spreading out beyond the glass
                   the garden
Lacks only this vase of roses.

7

At the window a jar of water
Into which have just been put
The Japanese paper flowers;

They have opened in less time
Than it takes to traverse
This awkward adjectival clause.

8

The elephant in the room
Is in fact an extremely gentle creature
Not in the least putting stress on a cane lounge
While it savours the many fond memories

Of former kindnesses it has enjoyed here with us.
In such novel and benign company
Tea may be served in the Meissen service
Since we are far from the china shop bull.

9

The tumbledown grass cliff leads to the sea
Down which no path follows singly
Without a zigzag. Unexpectedly

The sea is still immensely available
No matter which descent one takes
And all routes lead away from our samovar.

10

Cicadas outside the art gallery
Are 'deafening', the adjective worthy
Of *The Dictionary of Accepted Ideas*.

Their treadwater threshwing noise
Effaces even the garden roses
By making the ear the only sense.

Even here behind glass
Beside an avenue of mown grass
And a wall of trees

They seem intent on pinning
Some simile or other – familiar
Or strange – to the air.

11

The comfort of cicadas
And their wall of sound

Like tea being poured
On an industrial scale –

One for each person
One for the pot

And one for the road –
Above which in clouds

In their tannic white noise
A spoon would stand up.

12

'The Romans possibly had cats as pets.'
Could this uncertainty

                             still floating

On etheric waves
Explain our present cat's unfocused look?

13

From a pool of light or similar cliché
Adjoining the elephant in the room
The cry of 'Eureka!' reaches us

And as we turn to look
An ancient gent stands in his tub,
Water draining back from limbs

As he acclaims the displacement effect
Which amounts to this –
As we are absorbed in the present,

Outside, a corresponding sluice and spray
And chorus of the past drains back
And for a moment floats and falls.

14

The reluctant geraniums
Are taking their time
To open their eyes;

Tea on the veranda cools
At an immeasurably
Faster rate. Outside

The day seems
In all its second-guessing
Not to be passing at all.

15

Even more 'arrested in time'
Is the print resting on an easel
Of the Pompeiian fresco of figs
Compared with which
Tea is cooling like lightning.

16

A pleasant veranda week
Watching Antonioni's *L'Avventura*
Without a fast forwarding device

But with endless pauses for tea.

17

Tea infuses as we recall
The difficult beauties of the Kennedy era

Including the old joke
'I slept once with Jackie Kennedy;
We were both at the première
Of Samuel Barber's *Antony and Cleopatra*.'

18

'What do you get
When you cross a sociologist
With the Mafia?' 'You get
An offer you can't understand.'

The efflorescence of this effusion
Is akin to the radiance
Of the garden from the veranda
An hour after rain.

19

The jug of milk, and cups and saucers
Argue for a better description of themselves,
One which would imply consciousness;

And there are other contenders
Organising themselves in the arbour
With an even more impressive CV.

20

Orange blossom honey with sediment clouds,
Alstroemeria throats, Quimper teacups,
Are all similarly characterised
By tear drops or commas
Or dots and dashes in the design.

The 'time space continuum' out there
Filling the air over the lawn
And continuously keeping divisions seamless
Scarcely seems to resort
To these Morse code urgencies.

21

Freshly squeezed orange juice
Almost as fresh as
'Freshly squeezed water'
(The advertisement for filters)
Is asking us cordially
As it stands in its glass
To estimate how long before
It begins to taste of cordial,

While outside in the garden
Amongst flume and flux and fusion
In the wavy breeze
And the little lissom curves of grass,
Oxidation has been raised already
To the power of n where $n \to \infty$

22

While one of us reads about Laforgue
And Leah Lee briefly married in London,
Another boldly eats a peach;

Outside in the tinsel air butterflies
Are positively (insistently) didactic
In proposing infinite paths from A to B.

23

Composers (Stravinsky, Sibelius and others)
Demanding family silence at table
When inspiration is infusing in the pot

Propose an attention which, while dutiful,
Even difficult, allows the eyes
To roam into rose and hydrangea gardens.

24

The monoprint as Degas and Cressida Campbell discovered it
In which an image is laid down on glass, perhaps
Only to be simplified, made more modest, even blurred
By an overlaid sheet of paper – suggests in some way,

But with complicated exceptions as beset any likeness,
The trope of tea taken in front of a mountain
Where light arrives just in time to be bounced
From snow peaks towards a veranda and a cup
Raised to calm and receptive lips.

25

Two kinds of clouds
Overlaid, taking the whole glade,
Escarpment and more, to sort out
Their differences: one resolutely cumulus
As if Pan's pipe had fallen into soapsuds;
One like an uncertain haze as if
Daphne were still breathing ozone
After her laurel conversion.

This double collation of cloud
Has appeared,
Surprisingly, just as tea is poured.

26

Evening still undergoing dusk
Is so articulate, replete and familiar,
We might even be taking tea

In a Berlin Woolwork house
With rose arbours, thatched roof,
Hollyhocks and a gravel path.

27

No goldfish bowl (Matisse),
No cat or small dog
At the extreme edge (Bonnard),
No women in afternoon tea hats (Bonnard),

Only a chair and table,
A Marimekko cloth from Finland,
Cups and tea plates,
Books all awaiting a second reading
And a view of the valley.

28

Washed sheets on the line
(Recalling Cocteau's difficulties
In keeping the sheets wet
While filming *La Belle et la Bête*)

Are filling the garden
And drying almost as quickly
As gardenias are turning yellow.

29

Nectarines tasting like waterfalls,
Pears tasting like forest walks –
Fruit is the poor man's synaesthesia
And the tea urn is our own Rosetta Stone.

30

With the simile distillery dismantled
And stored in a garden shed
The air is so very clear
That swallows are drawn into its vacuum.

31

The swallows make elliptical arcs;
Tea is poured; the future is at last
Invited to step forward.

32

With the air outside so very clear
As if a vacuum
Were erasing traces of the past,
The tea being poured spirals and sways
While the swallows skim without resistance.

33

Although marked 'Chelsea England', a negligible mark
Scarcely traceable in standard texts,

The yellow tea cups are exactly the yellow
Of Worcester and Meissen canaries

In the collection of Mrs Gubbay
Now at Clandon House near Dorking, Surrey

And also in the Bowes Museum, Barnard Castle,
In the former collection of the formidable

Lady 'Birdie' Ludlow who, one morning
Chatting to the not-yet-Queen-Mother,

Said, 'I would like to collect porcelain. Why not?'
And went on to amass 600 items.

Although marked 'Chelsea England', a trivial mark
Which nonetheless suggests rich heritage,

The yellow teacups evoke former greatness
As a fragrant tea cools in them.

34

The glazed veranda
Acting like a hothouse
Has made the geraniums flower –

Although it would be pleasant
To attribute this gaiety
To an effusion derived

From row after row of books
On this same veranda –
And its duck-egg-blue cups and saucers.

35

The Pompeiian frescos of birds and figs,
Poggio discovering the lost manuscript of Lucretius,
An ancient gent standing in a shower of Eurekas,
Geraniums, a goldfish bowl, cicadas,
A cyclorama of swooping parrots –

All join hands walking forward
With a cast of thousands to proclaim *Now!*

36

With the pouring of tea,
The end of an era.

That is, all our yesterdays
Including the most recent –

All of the past
With the exception of today

Which even with 'Now'
Is in a holding pattern

Backed up against
Last night's curtains –

Here and now, in blue-and-white
With tea calmly cooling,

Is (or are) only just present
If soon to be mobilised

And transported backwards
Into its partly lit hangar.

Here in full light
It is as if 'space',

Always elusive,
Were no more

Than 'time' wrapped in a shawl
Of the very recent past.

With the pouring of tea
And the concerted clamour

In the garden of lorikeets,
The end of an era.

In Cumbria

A sentimental novel in 56 chapters

Foreword

A month after the German surrender in 1945
Kurt Schwitters, arch-Dadaist, moved to Ambleside.
He was accompanied by Edith Thomas,
A young woman half his age who had been
A Marks and Spencer telephonist. They had met
In his Paddington lodgings. He was by then already
Refusing to speak German and becoming English
By learning obsessively to drink tea.

Edith adored him and made tea so well
That he called her Wantee. She called him Jumbo.
They lived on almost no money, supplemented
By first and second prize at the annual
Ambleside and District Show Flower Painting Competition.

He was unknown in the Lake District; his performances
In Merz evenings at Hanover at which he declaimed
In puns, onomatopoeia, dog barking impressions,
Howling, growling and guttural insults,
Were quite unheard of there. And his collection
Of flotsam and discarded objects which would be used
In several more Merz towers continued unabated –
Assisted by generous replenishments of tea.

Four words, 'Want tea?' 'Yes, please.'

Forward with scissors and paste,
Fuelled by tea,
He cuts up the *Cumbria Bugle*.

Not a night passed in which he
Did not wake and want tea.

Wantee: 'Want tea?' 'Please. Darjeeling.'
'Once more with feeling?' 'And lemon.'

The next day was often almost identical
With the previous day.

Except that the clouds were entirely different,
Being like anvils rather than
Broderie anglaise supper cloths
Or Merz towers made from mosquito net.

Wantee: 'And furthermore, I note
That today the sun takes a more
Advantageous vantage above the yew.'

An automobile drew up
Outside the Ambleside Tea Rooms.

And alighting, a stranger ambled to the door.
Jumbo heard the bell and saw

Miss Cavendish greeting her customer
Against a mysterious sunset flare.

'Woof! Miaow!'

Variations on ululation. Vocal experiments.
The gargle investigated. Tea found unsuitable.

Wantee took down the willow pattern teapot.

A year before, in 1944,
During the opening of his first English exhibition,
While Wantee was still Miss Edith Thomas,
And Schwitters still Mr Jitters,
Word reached him that his wife
Had died in Hanover.

J: '*Dear Diary*, Today is identical with yesterday
Except for a slight breeze;
Yesterday had resembled the past
Which in general is calm.'

While travelling in Cumbria
At Dove Cottage he had seen
A tea caddy which, apparently,
Old William had apostrophised in a poem.

Little of this poem remained
Having been progressively the target
Of souvenir snippers like Schwitters.

So that by now only one word,
The opening apostrophe, remained:
'Yon…'

Wantee poured a delightful So Long Oolong tea,
As refreshing as sailing out to sea.

And Jumbo, practising
His colloquial English,
Sang, 'Wantee! How long you gonna be gone?'

As his English improved
He enjoyed the celebrated Cockney alphabet:
> A for 'orses
> B for mutton
> C for miles…

And he made a collection of English idioms,
Often wondering at their syntax.
For example how did
'Hail fellow well met' work?

One day over tea he remarked,
'Were this German it would be written
"Hailfellowwellmet"'.

And one day cutting this up
He mused over its anagram,
Wee ill? Fallow helmet?

As Wantee steps out
Into the yard with the laundry basket
He calls after her:
'You make heavenly tea,
With constellations of stars.'

On one of those days pleasantly
Indistinguishable from others
He woke to rose-hip tea
And afterwards a hip bath.

Miss Cavendish, 'My brother is here on a visit.'

Miss Cavendish claimed
To be distantly descended from Wordsworth.
J: 'Via the French Revolution?'

Miss Cavendish: 'It is mid-morning.
You should be ordering coffee.'
Jumbo: 'I prefer tea.'

A crisis soon resolved:
Miss Cavendish's brother,
Through a misunderstanding, confronted Jumbo
In the tea rooms. 'A word, Sir!'
At which, smiling, he did not demur.

'I believe you have appropriated
One of my valuable Mauritius stamps,
Somehow in your large collage
On display in the college.'

The next morning, 'It was all a mistake.
I apologise. I mistook
A photograph for the original.
It was all a storm in a teacup.'

Economies proving necessary,
Wantee bought broken biscuits
In large quantities from the school tuck-shop.

Jumbo was pleased to find
His favourite Oatmeal Surprise in the mix.

One morning fortune smiled on them.
Overnight on their front lawn
A crate of tea had fallen off the back of a truck
And, what's more, a large cake.

An idiom Jumbo found puzzling was this,
'He allowed it to pass through to the keeper.'

Jumbo mused, 'Many simple pursuits,
Which might be rich sources of speculation,
Remain quite neglected.
Dipping biscuits in tea is one.'

Cycling back from Dove Cottage,
Jumbo considered the art of collage,
'Cutting and pasting we lay waste our powers.'

While cutting up the *Cumbria Bugle* for collages
Wantee said, 'I see an elephant
Has given birth in captivity on the same day
A Zeppelin was caught in a tree
And rationing restrictions were eased.'

J: 'So that we will be
Allowed by decree
To dip more biscuits in more tea.'

One night Jumbo performed his variations
On Wordsworth's tea caddy poem,
Sonic variations on the word 'yon'.
Wantee had contributed 'won-ton' and 'bon-ton'
And after a visit to the Ambleside Bijou Cinema,
Rin Tin Tin.

Jumbo frequently repeated
The famous remark from *Punch*,
'Steward, if this is tea, please bring me some coffee;
But if this is coffee, I would like tea,'
While savouring his own Darjeeling.

Wantee (reading): 'When Tennyson visited Lyme Regis
He said, "Don't talk to me of the Duke of Monmouth.
Show me the exact spot where Louisa Musgrove fell!"'
Jumbo had never heard of *Persuasion*.

A poem:
Not a night passed
In which he did not wake
And want tea.

A mope:
In the severe winter of 1947
They spent long hours 'bundling' to keep warm –
While pouring tea with mittened hands.

An irony:
When Jumbo died in 1948
Wantee's collection of teapots was dispersed.
One remained unsold in an Elterwater antique shop
Until, twenty years later, it was bought
By the Ambleside Show Flower Painting Prize
Ladies' Catering Committee.

Jumbo's will leaving all his work to Wantee
Was contested – successfully –
By his son in Norway.

Wantee returned to London and became
Once more Miss Edith Thomas, manageress
Of an employment agency – there being, alas,
No opening for an extraordinary tea maker.

'Jasmine tea! Wonderful!'

In the tea shop. Jumbo: 'I am considering
Climbing Coleridge's mountain.'
Miss Cavendish: 'You'll need goggles. And toggles.'
Wantee giggles. 'And you'll be in the *Bugle*.'
Miss Cavendish: 'And there are eagles.'
A stranger: 'But no beagles.'
Another stranger: 'In the words of Hegel,
The mind may well prove to boggle.'

Jumbo walked to Windemere.
Falling into conversation with a complete stranger,
He said, 'I have an adorable tea-maker.'
Stranger: 'Edith Thomas?'

Another poem:
Not a night passed
In which he did not
Wake and want tea.

Their lawn with its concrete bird bath
And two wicker chairs by the path
Was ideal for afternoon tea.
Privacy was afforded by the ancient yew tree.

One day when using their willow pattern cups
Jumbo said, 'Let us imagine the story:
My dear companion is crossing the water;
Miss Cavendish is bringing us a collection
Of bus tickets, advertisement placards, film star pictures,
Cigarette cards, franked stamps, ration cards;
A senior Marks and Spencer telephonist is calling you back
But you are hiding behind these willows;
The Ambleside Show Flower Painting Prize
Judging Committee is crossing the bridge with their verdict;
A tea merchant is unloading tea.'

J: 'As I've often explained 'Merz' came from a scrap
Of newspaper with portion of the name Commerzbank.'
Wantee: 'Here in the *Cumbria Bugle*
Is that piece about a zeppelin.
Could you make Zepp poems?'
Jumbo: 'Miaow! Woof!'

Jumbo: 'How pleasant here in limbo.'

www.ingramcontent.com/pod-product-compliance
Lightning Source LLC
Chambersburg PA
CBHW062153100526
44589CB00014B/1815